|| श्रीः ||

|| निर्गुणमानसपूजा ||

śrīḥ

Nirguṇa-Mānasa-Pūjā

The Holy Worship of the Attributeless One in the Mind

by

śrī ādi śaṅkarācārya

Translated into English by
Dr. H. Ramamoorthy and Nome

© Society of Abidance in Truth
First edition 1993
Second edition 2024

ISBN 978-1-947154-35-3

Published by
Society of Abidance in Truth
1834 Ocean Street
Santa Cruz, California 95060
USA
www.satramana.org

Contents

ॐ श्री आदिशङ्कराचार्याय नमः

om śrī ādiśaṅkarācāryāya namaḥ

Introduction

ॐ

Puja is worship. What is worship? However performed, worship always involves the diminution or dissolution of the ego, which is the false assumption of existing as a separate individual. It is the cessation of the superimposition of individuality upon the real Existence, which is the Self. The definitions attributed to God correlate to the definitions attributed to oneself. In the Knowledge of the Self is found the revelation of the true nature of God, and herein lies the supreme worship of the Supreme, Brahman. As the Supreme Brahman is attributeless, so is the worship.

In 33 profound verses, cast as a dialogue between a guru and a disciple, Adi Sankaracarya simultaneously reveals the supreme knowledge of the Self and the highest devotional worship in this *Nirguna-Manasa-Puja, the Worship of the Attributeless One in the Mind*. That this puja in the mind is not the mere mental visualization of the upacaras, the steps or modes of worship, but is the apex of Brahman-Knowledge, is clearly evident throughout all of the verses. Verses 10 and 23 explicitly declare that the puja is to Siva and what the true nature of Siva is. That Siva is the Self is proclaimed again and again, by reference to the Atma-linga in verses 12, 15, 18, 22, 27, 29, and 32.

Sri Sankara's *Nirguna-Manasa-Puja* resembles, at least in the theme of a puja of nondualistic Knowledge, the statements ascribed to Suta as they appear in the Sanskrit *Ribhu Gita*, verses 3:46 and 3:47. This similarity is evident in the words of Ribhu in the *Song of Ribhu* (Tamil *Ribhu Gita*), verses 3:27 through 3:41. The resemblance also appears, perhaps to less of a degree, in the *Mandalabrahmana-Upanishad*. Speaking of death becoming upasecanam, a sprinkling of a condiment, by Sri Sankara in verse 21, correlates to the same declaration in the *Katha Upanishad*.

By reading and meditating upon these illuminative verses by Adi Sankara, one will experience this profound, supreme puja. May all who read these sacred verses be immersed in blissful Self-Knowledge and be ever absorbed in perpetual worship in the blemishless, space-like temple of pure Being, the Self.

Acknowledgements

There is much appreciation of and gratitude to Sasvati, Raman Muthukrishnan, Sangeeta Raman, and Ganesh Sadasivan for typing, proofreading, layout and design, and book distribution, and all who, in their generosity, support SAT publications and the SAT Temple.

Verse 1

शिष्य उवाच –
अखण्डे सच्चिदानन्दे
निर्विकल्पैकरूपिणि।
स्थितेऽद्वितीयभावेऽपि
कथं पूजा विधीयते ॥१॥

śiṣya uvāca -
akhaṇḍe saccidānande
nirvikalpaikarūpiṇi
sthite'dvitīyabhāve'pi
kathaṁ pūjā vidhīyate

śiṣya uvāca the disciple said **akhaṇḍe** in the undivided **saccidānande** in the Existence-Consciousness-Bliss **nirvikalpa eka rūpiṇi** in the one nature devoid of misconceptions (undifferentiated) **sthite advitīyabhāve api** even when (though) remaining in the non-dual (one without a second) state **kathaṁ pūjā vidhīyate** how is worship prescribed?

The disciple asked:

What manner of worship is prescribed in the undivided Existence-Consciousness-Bliss, in the one undifferentiated nature, though remaining in the state that is one without a second?

Verse 2

पूर्णस्यावाहनं कुत्र
सर्वाधारस्य चासनम्।
स्वच्छस्य पाद्यमर्घ्यं च
शुद्धस्याचमनं कुतः ॥२॥

pūrṇasyāvāhanaṁ kutra
sarvādhārasya cāsanam
svacchasya pādyamarghyaṁ ca
śuddhasyācamanaṁ kutaḥ

pūrṇasya āvāhanaṁ kutra where is [to be done] the invocation of the perfect, full, and complete **sarvādhārasya ca āsanam** and [where] the seat for the one who is the support of all **svacchasya** for the one who is pure, transparent, clear **pādyam arghyaṁ ca** [water] for feet washing and respectful libation **śuddhasya ācamanaṁ kutaḥ** wherefore the sips of water for the pure one

In what manner is the invocation to be done for the full, complete, and perfect One, and what is the seat to be offered for the one who is the support of all? Wherefore is the water for washing the feet and the respectful libation for the one who is clear and pure, and wherefore the sips of water for the immaculately pure?

Verse 3

निर्मलस्य कुतः स्नानं
वासो विश्वोदरस्य च।
अगोत्रस्य त्ववर्णस्य
कुतस्तस्योपवीतकम् ॥३॥

nirmalasya kutaḥ snānaṁ
vāso viśvodarasya ca
agotrasya tvavarṇasya
kutastasyopavītakam

nirmalasya of the blemishless, **kutaḥ snānaṁ** wherefore the bath **vāso viśvodarasya ca** and the garment of the one who holds the universe in his belly **agotrasya tu** of the one without a lineage, indeed **avarṇasya** of the one without a caste **kutaḥ tasya upavītakam** wherefore, for him, the sacred thread

Wherefore is the ablution of the blemishless and the garment of one who holds the universe in his belly? For one who has no family lineage (from rishis) and no caste, wherefore are the [triple strands of] the sacred thread?

Verse 4

निर्लेपस्य कुतो गन्धः
    पुष्पं निर्वासनस्य च।
निर्विशेषस्य का भूषा
    कोऽलंकारो निराकृतेः ॥४॥

nirlepasya kuto gandhaḥ
puṣpaṁ nirvāsanasya ca
nirviśeṣasya kā bhūṣā
ko'laṁkāro nirākṛteḥ

nirlepasya of the stainless (un-anointed) **kutaḥ gandhaḥ** wherefore the fragrance (sandal paste, candana) (to anoint) **puṣpaṁ ca** and flowers, **nirvāsanasya** of one without scents (tendencies of the past) **nirviśeṣasya** of one without any distinguishing features **kā bhūṣā** what is the adornment **kaḥ alaṁkāraḥ nirākṛteḥ** what beautification (decoration) for the formless

Wherefore are the sandal paste (fragrance) for the stainless one free from anointments and flowers for one free of vasanas (scents, tendencies)? What is the adornment of one without distinguishing features? What is the decoration for the formless?

Verse 5

निरञ्जनस्य किं धूपै-
दीपैर्वा सर्वसाक्षिणः।
निजानन्दैकतृप्तस्य
नैवेद्यं किं भवेदिह ॥५॥

nirañjanasya kiṁ dhūpai-
r-dīpairvā sarvasākṣiṇaḥ
nijānandaikatṛptasya
naivedyaṁ kiṁ bhavediha

nirañjanasya of the untainted **kiṁ dhūpaiḥ** what is the incense **dīpaiḥ vā** or of lights **sarvasākṣiṇaḥ** for the witness of all **nija ānanda eka tṛptasya** of the one satisfied in his own bliss **naivedyaṁ kiṁ bhaved iha** what shall be the food offering here

What is the waving of incense before the taintless or the waving of light for one who is the witness of all? What shall be the food offering here for one who is completely satisfied with his own Bliss?

Verse 6

विश्वानन्दयितुस्तस्य
किं ताम्बूलं प्रकल्पते।
स्वयंप्रकाशचिद्रूपो
योऽसावर्कादिभासकः ॥६॥

viśvānandayitustasya
kiṁ tāmbūlaṁ prakalpate
svayaṁprakāśacidrūpo
yo'sāvarkādi bhāsakaḥ

viśva ānandayituḥ tasya for him who makes the universe happy (blissful) **kiṁ tāmbūlaṁ prakalpate** what betel leaf (pack) is considered proper **svayaṁ prakāśa** one who is self-luminous **cid rūpaḥ** of the nature of Consciousness **yaḥ asau** he who **arka ādi bhāsakaḥ** is the illuminator of the sun and such

What is designated as the betel leaf for the one who makes the universe blissful? For one who is self-luminous, of the nature of Consciousness, and is the illuminator of the sun and other [luminaries],

Verse 7

गीयते श्रुतिभिस्तस्य
नीराजनविधिः कुतः।
प्रदक्षिणमनन्तस्य
प्रणामोऽद्वयवस्तुनः॥७॥
or
प्रमाणोऽद्वयवस्तुनः॥७॥

gīyate śrutibhistasya
nīrājanavidhiḥ kutaḥ
pradakṣiṇamanantasya
praṇāmo'dvayavastunaḥ
or
pramāṇo'dvayavastunaḥ

gīyate śrutibhiḥ tasya of him who is glorified (praised) by the Vedas **nīrājana vidhiḥ kutaḥ** wherefore the ritual (rule, precept, direction, mode of action) of camphor-waving **pradakṣiṇam anantasya** circumambulation of the limitless (infinite) **praṇāmaḥ advaya vastunaḥ** prostration for the nondual Reality or **pramāṇaḥ advaya vastunaḥ** the proof of the non-dual reality

what is the mode of camphor light offering for one who is glorified by the Vedas? Wherefore is the circumambulation of the one who is endless and the prostration for the nondual Reality (of the one who is the proof of non-dual Truth)?

Verse 8

वेदवाचामवेद्यस्य
   किं वा स्तोत्रं विधीयते।
अन्तर्बहिः संस्थित-
   स्योद्वासनविधिः कुतः॥८॥

vedavācāmavedyasya
kiṁ vā stotraṁ vidhīyate
antarbahiḥ saṁsthita-
syodvāsanavidhiḥ kutaḥ

veda vācām avedyasya of the one who cannot be comprehended by the words of the Vedas **kiṁ vā stotraṁ vidhīyate** what indeed is the song of praise (eulogy) prescribed **antarbahiḥ saṁsthitasya** of one who is established both inside and outside **udvāsana vidhiḥ kutaḥ** wherefore the ritual (precept, mode of action) of sending away (leave-taking) after worship

What is the song of praise prescribed for praising the one who cannot be comprehended through the words of the Vedas? What is the way (ritual) of bidding goodbye to one who exists both inside and outside?

Verse 9

श्री गुरुरुवाच-
आराधयामि मणिसंनिभमात्मलिङ्गं
मायापुरीहृदयपङ्कजसंनिविष्टम्।
श्रद्धानदीविमलचित्तजलाभिषेकै-
र्नित्यं समाधिकुसुमैरपुनर्भवाय॥९॥

śrī gururuvāca-
ārādhayāmi maṇisaṁnibhamātmaliṅgaṁ
māyāpurīhṛdayapaṅkajasaṁniviṣṭam
śraddhānadīvimalacittajalābhiṣekai-
r-nityaṁ samādhikusumairapunarbhavāya

śrī guruḥ uvāca the revered Guru said (replied), **ārādhayāmi** I worship **maṇi saṁnibham** the bejeweled (resembling a jewel) **ātma liṅgaṁ** linga of the Self **māyāpurī hṛdaya paṅkaja saṁniviṣṭam** seated in the city of maya (the illusory body) the heart-lotus **śraddhā nadī vimala citta jala abhiṣekaiḥ** by ablutions in the clear water of thought (stainless mind) in the river (current) of faith **nityaṁ** always (daily, ever) **samādhi kusumaiḥ** by the flowers of samadhi **apunar bhavāya** for not being born again

The revered Guru replied:

I worship the bejeweled linga of the Self, residing in the city of maya, the lotus of the heart of the illusory body, by the sacred ablution of the clear water of thought in the river of faith and ever by the flowers of samadhi for not being born again.

Verse 10

अयमेकोऽवशिष्टोऽस्मी-
त्येवमावाहयेच्छिवम्।
आसनं कल्पयेत्पश्चा-
त्स्वप्रतिष्ठात्मचिन्तनम् ॥१०॥

ayameko'vaśiṣṭo'smī-
t-yevamāvāhayecchivam
āsanaṁ kalpayetpaścā-
t-svapratiṣṭhātmacintanam

ayam ekaḥ this one (alone) **avaśiṣṭaḥ asmi** I am the remaining **iti evam āvāhayet śivam** thus, indeed, should Siva be invoked **āsanaṁ kalpayet** the seat should then be formed **paścāt** thereafter **svapratiṣṭha** established in oneself **ātma cintanam** the thought of the Self

I am the only one remaining—thus is Siva to be invoked. Thereafter, the thought of the Self established in oneself should be formed (offered) as the seat.

Verse 11

पुण्यपापरजःसङ्गो
मम नास्तीति वेदनम् ।
पाद्यं समर्पयेद्विद्वा-
न्सर्वकल्मषनाशनं ॥११॥

puṇyapāparajaḥ saṅgo
mama nāstīti vedanam
pādyaṁ samarpayedvidvā-
n-sarvakalmaṣanāśanam

puṇya pāpa rajaḥ saṅgaḥ connection to (association with) the dust of sin and merit **mama nāsti** is not for me (my) **iti vedanaṁ** a perception (knowledge) thus **pādyaṁ samarpayet vidvān** the learned (wise) one should offer [as] water for feet-washing **sarva kalmaṣa nāśanaṁ** which does away with (is the removal of) all impurities

There is no connection for me with the dust of merit or demerit—perceiving thus, the wise one should offer water for washing of the feet that removes all impurities.

Verse 12

अनादिकल्पविधृत-
मूलाज्ञानजलाञ्जलिम् ।
विसृजेदात्मलिङ्गस्य
तदेवार्घ्यसमर्पणम् ॥१२॥

anādikalpavidhṛta-
mūlājñānajalāñjalim
visṛjedātmaliṅgasya
tadevārghyasamarpaṇam

anādi kalpa vidhṛtam carried (possessed) practically (equal to) an eon, origin-less **mūla ajñāna** the primal ignorance **jalāñjalim visṛjet** the salutation with water should be poured down **ātma liṅgasya** of the linga of the Self **tat eva** that indeed **arghya samarpaṇaṁ** is the offering of respectful libation

Pouring of the water of primal ignorance, which is practically origin-less and has been carried for eons, on the linga of the Self is, indeed, the offering of the respectful libation.

Verse 13

ब्रह्मानन्दाब्धिकल्लोल-
कणकोट्यंशलेशकम् ।
पिबन्तीन्द्रादय इति
ध्यानमाचमनं मतम् ॥१३॥

brahmānandābdhikallola-
kaṇakoṭyaṁśaleśakam
pibantīndrādaya iti
dhyānamācamanaṁ matam

brahma ānanda abdhi kallola a wave in the ocean of Brahman-Bliss **kaṇa koṭi aṁśa leśakaṁ** the slightest part of a particle of a millionth part of a drop **pibanti indrādaya** Indra (the chief of gods) and others drink (enjoy) **iti dhyānam ācamanaṁ mataṁ** this meditation is considered the offering of sips of water

The meditation that Indra and others drink of only a tiny drop of a millionth part of the billows of the ocean of Brahman-Bliss is understood to be the offering of the sips of water.

Verse 14

ब्रह्मानन्दजलेनैव
 लोकाःसर्वे परिप्लुताः।
अच्छेद्योऽयमिति ध्यान-
 मभिषेचनमात्मनः ॥१४॥

brahmānandajalenaiva
lokāḥ sarve pariplutāḥ
acchedyo'yamiti dhyāna-
m-abhiṣecanam ātmanaḥ

brahma ānanda jalena eva indeed by the waters of the Brahman-Bliss **lokāḥ sarve** all the worlds **pariplutāḥ** are flooded **acchedyaḥ ayam** this is indivisible **iti dhyānam** meditation thus **abhiṣecanam ātmanaḥ** the ablution (anointing) of the Self

All of the worlds are, indeed, flooded with the waters of Brahman-Bliss. The meditation thus that this is (I am) indivisible is the sacred ablution for the Self.

Verse 15

निरावरणचैतन्यं
प्रकाशोऽस्मीति चिन्तनम् ।
आत्मलिङ्गस्य सद्वस्त्र-
मित्येवं चिन्तयेन्मुनिः ॥१५॥

nirāvaraṇa caitanyaṁ
prakāśo'smīti cintanam
ātmaliṅgasya sadvastra-
m-ityevaṁ cintayenmuniḥ

nirāvaraṇa caitanyaṁ the sentience (Consciousness, Supreme Spirit) without any veiling **prakāśaḥ asmi** I am radiant (effulgent, shining, luminous) **iti cintanam** thinking (considering) thus **ātmaliṅgasya sadvastram** is the true garment of the linga of the Self **iti evaṁ cintayet muniḥ** the sage should reflect thus

I am the light of Consciousness without any veil. Considering thus is the true draping of a garment for the linga of the Self. Thus should the sage reflect.

Verse 16

त्रिगुणात्माशेषलोक-
मालिकासूत्रमस्म्यहम् ।
इति निश्चयमेवात्र
ह्युपवीतं परं मतम् ॥१६॥

triguṇātmāśeṣaloka-
mālikāsūtramasmyaham
iti niścayamevātra
hyupavītaṁ paraṁ matam

triguṇātmā comprising (of the nature of) the triple [strands of] qualities (guṇa-s) **aśeṣa loka mālikā** of the garland of worlds without end (without remainder, entire) **sūtram asmi aham** I am the thread that runs through **iti niścayam eva atra** a certitude thus here indeed **hi upavītaṁ paraṁ matam** is surely considered the supreme sacred thread

The certitude that I am the thread that runs through the garland of the entire world of the triple [strands of] qualities is, indeed, here surely understood to be the supreme sacred thread.

Verse 17

अनेकवासनामिश्र-
प्रपञ्चोऽयं धृतो मया ।
नान्येनेत्यनुसंधान-
मात्मनश्चन्दनं भवेत् ॥१७॥

anekavāsanāmiśra-
prapañco'yaṁ dhṛto mayā
nānyenetyanusaṁdhāna-
m-ātmanaścandanaṁ bhavet

aneka vāsanā misraḥ prapañcaḥ ayaṁ this manifest world with the mixture of numerous scents (tendencies) **dhṛtaḥ mayā** is supported (held, possessed, worn) by me **na anyena** not by anyone else (another) **iti anusaṁdhānam** an inquiry, thus **ātmanaḥ candanaṁ bhavet** will be the [fragrant] sandal paste of the Self

The inquiry that this manifest world with the mixture of numerous mixed scents (tendencies) is supported by me and by none else will be the [fragrant] sandal paste for the Self.

Verse 18

रजःसत्त्वतमोवृत्ति-
त्यागरूपैस्तिलाक्षतैः ।
आत्मलिङ्गं यजेन्नित्यं
जीवन्मुक्तिप्रसिद्धये ॥१८॥

rajaḥsattvatamovṛtti-
tyāgarūpaistilākṣataiḥ
ātmaliṅgaṁ yajennityaṁ
jīvanmuktiprasiddhaye

rajaḥ sattvaḥ tamaḥ vṛttiḥ tyāgarūpaiḥ in the form of the renunciation (abandonment) of the modes of the equipoised (good, wise, existent, purity), the energetic (passionate, excited), and the dull (darkness, gloom) (sattva, rajas, tamas) **tila akṣataiḥ** [as] sesame and unbroken rice grains **ātmaliṅgaṁ yajet nityaṁ** the linga of the Self should be worshipped ever **jīvanmukti prasiddhaye** for the full attainment of liberation while yet alive

With the abandonment of the diverse modes of rajas, sattva, and tamas, as sesame seeds and unbroken rice grains, the linga of the Self should ever be worshipped for the full attainment of liberation while alive (jivanmukti).

Verse 19

ईश्वरो गुरुरात्मेति
भेदत्रयविवर्जितैः ।
बिल्वपत्रैरद्वितीयै-
रात्मलिङ्गं यजेच्छिवम् ॥१९॥

īśvaro gururātmeti
bhedatrayavivarjitaiḥ
bilva patrair advitīyai-
r-ātmaliṅgaṁ yajecchivam

īśvaraḥ guruḥ ātmā iti Isvara (the Lord, God), Guru, and the Self, thus **bhedatraya vivarjitaiḥ** devoid of a three-fold difference **bilvapatraiḥ** with bilva leaves **advitīyaiḥ** of non-duality (without a second) **ātmaliṅgaṁ yajet śivam** one should worship the peaceful (auspicious, benevolent) linga of the Self (Siva, the Self-linga)

One should worship the auspicious, peaceful linga of the Self with bilva leaves that are devoid of the triple differentiation of the Lord, the Guru, and the Self and that are without a second.

Verse 20

समस्तवासनात्यागं
धूपं तस्य विचिन्तयेत् ।
ज्योतिर्मयात्मविज्ञानं
दीपं संदर्शयेद्बुधः ॥२०॥

samastavāsanātyāgaṁ
dhūpaṁ tasya vicintayet
jyotirmayātmavijñānaṁ
dīpaṁ saṁdarśayedbudhaḥ

samasta vāsanā tyāgaṁ the renunciation (abandonment) of all scents (tendencies) **dhūpaṁ** incense offering **tasya** of him **vicintayet** one should think of (discern, consider) **jyotirmaya** full of light **ātmavijñānaṁ** the knowledge of the Self **dīpaṁ** the offering of the lighted wick (lamp) **saṁdarśayet budhaḥ** the wise one should show (wave in front, display, see)

The renunciation of all tendencies should be considered as the incense offering to Him. The wise one should display (wave) the lighted lamp of the luminous Knowledge of the Self.

Verse 21

नैवेद्यमात्मलिङ्गस्य
ब्रह्माण्डाख्यं महोदनम् ।
पिबानन्दरसं स्वादु
मृत्युरस्योपसेचनम् ॥२१॥

naivedyamātmaliṅgasya
brahmāṇḍākhyaṁ mahodanam
pibānandarasaṁ svādu
mṛtyurasyopasecanam

naivedyam ātmaliṅgasya the food offering for the linga of the Self **brahmāṇḍākhyaṁ mahodanam** the massive cooked food [offering] known as the cosmic Brahman egg **pibānanda rasaṁ svādu** the essence of bliss is the relishable (sweet, delightful) drink **mṛtyuḥ asya upasecanam** death [itself] is a condiment (sprinkling, pouring) of this

The massive cooked rice offering (naivedya) for the atma-linga is the cosmos known as the Brahman-egg. The essence of Bliss is the sweet, delightful drink. Death, itself, is the condiment sprinkled on this [cooked food].

Verse 22

अज्ञानोच्छिष्टकरस्य
क्षालनं ज्ञानवारिणा ।
विशुद्धस्यात्मलिङ्गस्य
हस्तप्रक्षालनं स्मरेत् ॥२२॥

ajñānocchiṣṭakarasya
kṣālanaṁ jñānavāriṇā
viśuddhasyātmaliṅgasya
hastaprakṣālanaṁ smaret

ajñāna ucchiṣṭakarasya of the hand with the polluted remains of ignorance **kṣālanaṁ jñāna vāriṇā** washing by the waters of knowledge **viśuddhasya ātmaliṅgasya** for the pure linga of the Self **hastaprakṣālanaṁ smaret** should be remembered (thought of, construed) as the hand washing

The hand washing should be construed as the washing of the hand polluted with the remains of ignorance by the waters of Knowledge for the pure linga of the Self.

Verse 23

रागादिगुणशून्यस्य
शिवस्य परमात्मनः ।
सरागविषयाभ्यास-
त्यागस्ताम्बूलचर्वणम् ॥२३॥

rāgādiguṇaśūnyasya
śivasya paramātmanaḥ
sarāgaviṣayābhyāsa-
tyāgastāmbūlacarvaṇam

rāgādi guṇa śūnyasya of one devoid of the qualities such as passion and others **śivasya paramātmanaḥ** of Siva the Supreme Self **sarāga viṣaya abhyāsa tyāgaḥ** the renunciation (abandonment) of the practice of passion for objects **tāmbūla carvaṇam** is the chewing of betel

The offering of betel, for chewing, to the Supreme Self, Siva, devoid of passion and other qualities, is the abandonment of the practice of passion for objects. (or: is the practice of renunciation of passion for objects.)

Verse 24

अज्ञानध्वान्तविध्वंस-
प्रचण्डमतिभास्करम् ।
आत्मनो ब्रह्मताज्ञानं
नीराजनमिहात्मनः ॥२४॥

ajñānadhvāntavidhvaṁsa-
pracaṇḍamatibhāskaram
ātmano brahmatājñānaṁ
nīrājanamihātmanaḥ

ajñāna dhvānta vidhvaṁsa the destruction of the darkness of ignorance **pracaṇḍa mati bhāskaram** the powerful (great, burning) illuminating, shining sun of intellect (understanding, determination, view) **ātmanaḥ brahmatā jñānaṁ** the knowledge of the Atman (the Self) being Brahman (the knowledge of oneself being Brahman) **nīrājanam iha ātmanaḥ** is here the waving of camphor light for the Self

The camphor light offering to the Self, here, is one's own Knowledge of Brahmanhood (is the Knowledge of the Self being Brahman), the understanding that, like the great, dazzling sun, destroys the darkness of ignorance.

Verse 25

विविधब्रह्मसंदृष्टि-
मालिकाभिरलंकृतम् ।
पूर्णानन्दात्मतादृष्टिं
पुष्पाञ्जलिमनुस्मरेत् ॥२५॥

vividhabrahmasaṁdṛṣṭi-
r-mālikābhiralaṁkṛtaṁ
pūrṇānandātmatādṛṣṭiṁ
puṣpāñjalimanusmaret

vividha brahma saṁdṛṣṭiḥ mālikābhiḥ alaṁkṛtaṁ adorned by the garlands of the perception of Brahman in various manifestations **pūrṇa ānanda ātmatā dṛṣṭiṁ** the perception of the Self as the perfect (full) Bliss **puṣpāñjalim anusmaret** should be remembered as the offering of flowers

One should remember the perception of Brahman in various forms as the adornment with garlands and the perception of the Self as full, perfect Bliss as the offering of [scattering of] flowers.

Verse 26

परिभ्रमन्ति ब्रह्माण्ड-
सहस्राणि मयीश्वरे ।
कूटस्थाचलरूपोऽह-
मिति ध्यानं प्रदक्षिणम् ॥२६॥

paribhramanti brahmāṇḍa-
sahasrāṇi mayīśvare
kūṭasthācalarūpo'ha-
m-iti dhyānaṁ pradakṣiṇam

paribhramanti brahmāṇḍa sahasrāṇi thousands of Brahman eggs (universes) revolve (wander) **mayi īśvare** in me, the Lord **kūṭastha acala rūpaḥ aham** I am of the nature of the Supreme, unmoving, immovable (unchangeable) **iti dhyānaṁ pradakṣiṇam** meditation thus is the circumambulation

Thousands of universes wander inside me, the Lord. I am of the nature of the Supreme, immovable, unchangeable, and motionless—this meditation is the circumambulation.

Verse 27

विश्ववन्द्योऽहमेवास्मि
नास्ति वन्द्यो मदन्यतः।
इत्यालोचनमेवात्र
स्वात्मलिङ्गस्य वन्दनम् ॥२७॥

viśvavandyo'hamevāsmi
nāsti vandyo madanyataḥ
ityālocanamevātra
svātmaliṅgasya vandanam

viśvavandyaḥ aham eva asmi I indeed am the one to whom the entire universe should make obeisance **na asti vandyaḥ** none there is to be bowed to **mat anyataḥ** apart from (other than) me **iti ālocanam eva atra** contemplating thus, indeed, here **su ātmaliṅgasya vandanam** is the obeisance to the excellent (exalted) linga of the Self

I alone am the one to whom the entire universe should make obeisance; apart from me, there is none else to whom to bow—contemplating thus is, indeed, the obeisance to the excellent linga of the Self.

Verse 28

आत्मनः सत्क्रिया प्रोक्ता
कर्तव्याभावभावना ।
नामरूपव्यतीतात्म-
चिन्तनं नामकीर्तनम् ॥२८॥

ātmanaḥ satkriyā proktā
kartavyābhāvabhāvanā
nāmarūpavyatītātma-
cintanaṁ nāmakīrtanam

ātmanaḥ satkriyā proktā the true activity (ritual) of the Self is said to be **kartavya abhāva bhāvanā** the bhava (conviction, attitude) that nothing exists to be done **nāma rūpa vyatīta** transcending (surpassing, pass beyond) name and form **ātma cintanaṁ** the thought (understanding) of the Self **nāma kīrtanam** the singing of the names

The true activity of the Self is declared to be the conviction that nothing exists to be done. The thought of the Self's transcendence of names and forms is the singing of the names [in worship].

Verse 29

श्रवणं तस्य देवस्य
श्रोतव्याभावचिन्तनम् ।
मननं त्वात्मलिङ्गस्य
मन्तव्याभावचिन्तनम् ॥२९॥

śravaṇaṁ tasya devasya
śrotavyābhāvacintanam
mananaṁ tvātmaliṅgasya
mantavyābhāvacintanam

śravaṇaṁ tasya devasya listening to that Lord (God, Deity) **śrotavya abhāva cintanam** is the thought (understanding) of the nonexistence of [anything] to be heard **mananaṁ tu ātmaliṅgasya** the mental reflection of the linga of the Self, too **mantavya abhāva cintanam** the thought (understanding, consideration) of the nonexistence of [anything] to be reflected upon (thought of)

Listening to that God (Deva) is the understanding of the nonexistence of anything to be heard. Reflection on the linga of the Self is the understanding of the nonexistence of anything upon which to reflect.

Verse 30

ध्यातव्याभावविज्ञानं
निदिध्यासनमात्मनः।
समस्तभ्रान्तिविक्षेप-
राहित्येनात्मनिष्ठता ॥३०॥

dhyātavyābhāvavijñānaṁ
nididhyāsanamātmanaḥ
samastabhrāntivikṣepa-
rāhityenātmaniṣṭhatā

dhyātavya abhāva vijñānaṁ the knowledge of the nonexistence of anything to be meditated upon **nididhyāsanam ātmanaḥ** is the profound meditation on the Self **samasta bhrānti vikṣepa rāhityena** by the freedom from false projection of all mental errors (by being without confusion) **ātma niṣṭhatā** is the abidance in the Self

The knowledge of the nonexistence of anything upon which to meditate is the profound meditation on the Self. By freedom from the false projection of all confusion, there is abidance in the Self.

Verse 31

समाधिरात्मनो नाम
नान्यच्चित्तस्य विभ्रमः।
तत्रैव ब्रह्मणि सदा
चित्तविश्रान्तिरिष्यते ॥३१॥

samādhirātmano nāma
nānyaccittasya vibhramaḥ
tatraiva brahmaṇi sadā
cittaviśrāntiriṣyate

samādhiḥ ātmanaḥ nāma what is named the samadhi of the Self **na anyat cittasya vibhramaḥ** is no (the absence of) mental error (confusion of the mind) of anything else [existing] **tatra eva brahmaṇi sadā** there, indeed, always [abiding] in Brahman **citta viśrāntiḥ iṣyate** is prescribed (proclaimed) as repose (coming to an end) of thought (the mind)

What is named the samadhi of the Self is no confusion of the mind of anything else being existent. There, indeed, repose of the mind is proclaimed to be abidance always in Brahman.

Verse 32

एवं वेदान्तकल्पोक्त
स्वात्मलिङ्गप्रपूजनम् ।
कुर्वन्नामरणं वापि
क्षणं वा सुसमाहितः ॥३२॥

evaṁ vedāntakalpokta
svātmaliṅgaprapūjanam
kurvannāmaraṇaṁ vāpi
kṣaṇaṁ vā susamāhitaḥ

evaṁ vedānta kalpa ukta thus, as spoken of in Vedantic cannon (sacred precept) **svātmaliṅga (su ātmaliṅga) prapūjanam kurvan** performing the worship of the linga of one's own Self (of the exalted (honored) linga of the Self) **āmaraṇaṁ kṣaṇaṁ vā api** until death or even for a moment **vā su samāhitaḥ** indeed extremely calm and collected

Thus, performing the worship of the exalted linga of one's own Self, as declared in the sacred precepts of Vedanta, all through life until death or for just a moment, with full composure, indeed,

Verse 33

सर्वदुर्वासनाजालं
    पदपांसुमिव त्यजेत् ।
विधूयाज्ञानदुःखौघं
    मोक्षानन्दं समश्नुते ॥३३॥

sarvadurvāsanājālaṁ
padapāṁsumiva tyajet
vidhūyājñānaduḥkhaughaṁ
mokṣānandaṁ samaśnute

sarva durvāsanā jālaṁ the net (snare, [tangled] web) of all bad tendencies **padapāṁsum iva tyajet** one should renounce (abandon) like the dust of the feet **vidhūya ajñāna duḥkha oghaṁ** cutting (shaking) off from oneself the sorrow (suffering) the stream (river) of ignorance **mokṣānandaṁ samaśnute** one enjoys (savors) well, the bliss of liberation

one should abandon the entire tangled web of all bad tendencies like the dust on the feet. Shaking off from oneself the sorrow-ridden stream of ignorance, one enjoys the bliss of Liberation.

इति श्रीमत्परमहंसपरिव्राजकाचार्यस्य
श्रीगोविन्दभगवत्पूज्यपादशिष्यस्य
श्रीमच्छंकरभगवतः कृतौ
निर्गुणमानसपूजा संपूर्णा ॥

iti śrīmat-paramahaṁsa-parivrājakācāryasya
śrī-govinda-bhagavat-pūjyapāda-śiṣyasya
śrīmacchaṁkara-bhagavataḥ kṛtau
nirguṇa-mānasa-pūjā saṁpūrṇā

Thus of the revered, holy, wandering recluse
and great spiritual teacher
Sri Govinda Bhagavan, whose feet are to be worshiped,
by the disciple, the revered, holy
Sankara Bhagavan composed,
Nirguṇa-Mānasa-Pūja concludes.

Appendix

Upacārā-s in Worship
(Courtesies and Honors in Pūja)

There are several courtesies and honors accorded to the deity in a puja or ritual worship. The numbers vary from about five to sixty-four and more according to the tradition practiced and details of worship. The same are extended mentally in mental worship. The various items dealt with in this text are:

Meditation	(dhyāna)
Invocation (in the icon or picture or otherwise)	(āvāhana)
Offering of seat	(āsana)
Water for feet washing	(pādya)
Respectful libation	(arghya)
Sips of water	(ācamana)
Formal ablution	(snāna)
Garments	(vastra)
Triple strand of sacred thread (over left shoulder and under right arm)	(upavīta)
Ornaments	(ābharaṇa)
Sandal paste	(candana)
Rice grains – unbroken	(akṣata)
Flowers	(puṣpa)
Incense	(dhūpa)
Light on a wick	(dīpa)
Cooked food	(naivedya)
Seasonings	(upasecana)

Water for hand washing	(hastaprakṣalana)
Betel leaves	(tāmbūla)
Scattering of flowers	(puṣpāñjali)
Waving of camphor light	(nīrājana)
Circumambulation (clockwise)	(pradakṣiṇa)
Prostration	(namaskāra)
Singing of names	(nāmakirtana)
Release (bidding good-bye)	(udvāsana)

www.ingramcontent.com/pod-product-compliance
Lightning Source LLC
Chambersburg PA
CBHW061806070526
44586CB00023B/2732
9781947154353